# The Path to Finding a Senior Living Community

# Table of Contents

# The Path to Finding a Senior Living Community

(Formerly published as 'Find the Perfect Retirement Community for You')

## Introduction

I began working with seniors and their families in 1987, when I worked as a caregiver at a retirement community. I fell in love with the residents and went on to obtain my Bachelor of Science degree in Gerontology and my Master of Science degree in Counseling Psychology. Years later, I further advanced my education and became a Certified Senior Advisor.

During all that time, I worked in various senior living communities as an Activity Director, Bookkeeper, Social Service Director, Executive Director/Administrator, Community Relations Director, and more. I'm the President/CEO of Age Boldly Consulting and my parents lived in a retirement community until recently. Needless to say, I've seen and experienced a lot in the senior health and housing industry. There have been some wonderful times and some awful, heart-breaking times. I wouldn't change it for anything.

Throughout my years in this industry, I've seen many people confused, anxious, and extremely stressed about looking for, choosing, and moving into a retirement community. People walk into a community and have no idea what they're looking for, what questions to ask, or how to take the process from start to finish.

I've written this book to help you through the process and to answer questions that you have. I've also included answers to some questions that you probably haven't thought to ask. This book will be full of helpful tips, questions to contemplate, things to look for, processes to follow, and so much more.

In this book, I'm using the terms senior living community, independent living community, retirement community, and assisted living community somewhat interchangeably. I'm also referencing rules/regulations in Washington State

# The Path to Finding a Senior Living Community

since that's where I live. Check with your local Home & Community Service (HCS) office for rules/regulations pertaining to your specific state.

I've also added some stories and tips from my many years in this industry. You'll find them in *italics* throughout this book.

# The Path to Finding a Senior Living Community

## When is it Time to Move?

There are so many options, more and more each day, available in the senior housing industry. Moving into a senior living community won't be the answer for everyone. How, then, does someone decide if it's the right move for them? Some things to consider are:

Would you enjoy living in an apartment;

Do you enjoy socializing with others;

Would you like to have someone available to assist you with tasks such as cooking, cleaning, transportation, home maintenance, medication management, etc. (or are you ready to give up those tasks completely);

Do you enjoy easy access to various forms of entertainment such as live music, outings, board and card games, special theme dinners, movies, educational speakers, etc.;

Would you like to make bill paying easier by combining your rent, utilities, food, transportation, maintenance, etc. into one monthly payment;

Do you need assistance with Activities of Daily Living (ADLs) such as medication management, bathing, dressing, transferring, etc.?

Let's look at each of these individually.

# The Path to Finding a Senior Living Community

*Would you enjoy living in an apartment?*

Retirement communities are basically apartment buildings that cater to people 62 years of age and older (some will allow younger people, so ask about the age requirements). For many people, moving to an apartment will mean downsizing from a home that they've lived in for quite a number of years. This can be very difficult, both physically and emotionally. However, it *can* be done, as proven by the many people who are happily living in retirement communities.

Some advantages of downsizing to a senior living community include saving money (you no longer need to pay for yard and home maintenance, property taxes, cable television, a housekeeper, etc.); it's less work for you (no more shoveling snow in the winter and raking leaves in the fall); you can leave on vacation and know that people are looking after your home for you; and you can diversify your investments (instead of your net worth being tied up in a home, you can use proceeds from the sale of your home to diversity your portfolio).

During my 30+ years working in the senior housing industry, I've hardly ever seen someone move in and exclaim, "I've reached my goal of living in senior housing!" However, the majority of people that move in do tell me, a few months after the move, that they don't know why they didn't make the move sooner. They now have time to enjoy life more, they're not overwhelmed by yard work and home maintenance, they have friends to socialize with, they're entertained with activities and events, they're enjoying nutritious food, and so much more.

# The Path to Finding a Senior Living Community

*I had one woman come to talk with me about moving into a retirement community. Part of my job was to ask her why she was considering a move. She proceeded to talk, non-stop (I didn't even see her take a breath!) about her husband, his life, her kids, their lives, etc. I finally interrupted her to ask her about herself, as she was the one looking to make a change. "Well," she said, "I have this birthmark on my cheek."*

*If you're talking with a professional about making a move, and they ask you about yourself and why you're considering a move, please don't talk about your birthmarks!*

### *Do you enjoy socializing with others?*

There are many studies available telling us that loneliness is very detrimental to our health. Humans are social creatures and need interaction with others. Perhaps no other age group experiences loneliness more than the elderly. As we age, changes we face contribute to a more solitary life. Our family may live far away from us, our friends are aging themselves and may become ill or pass away, friends who do live close by may be inaccessible due to decreased mobility, bad vision and hearing loss can make it difficult to communicate, we may avoid others due to embarrassment about our physical problems (incontinence, oxygen therapy, the need for a walker or wheelchair), etc.

A University of California, San Francisco (UCSF) study found that participants 60 years old and older who reported feeling lonely saw a 45 percent increase in their risk of death.

Living in a retirement community means that you'll have many people in your age group living near you in the same community. For many, this is a wonderful opportunity! I've had family members come to me and tell me that their mom,

# The Path to Finding a Senior Living Community

grandma, dad, or grandpa lives alone at home and just sits around watching TV all day. They're lonely, depressed, aren't eating well, aren't taking their medications properly, aren't cleaning the house or keeping up with the yard work, and aren't enjoying life the way that they used to. In a retirement community, you have the opportunity to create new friendships, try new activities, once again participate in activities that you used to enjoy, discover new hobbies, and return to enjoying your life.

*A good marketer will usually ask you if you want to leave a deposit for an apartment. Don't be shocked or offended by this question. You're looking at a retirement community for a reason, and that reason is because you're considering a move. Maybe you're not planning to move for a year or more, but you can still put a deposit down on a wait list. Have a checkbook or credit card with you just in case the perfect apartment is there – you don't want to lose out because you weren't prepared!*

*Would you like to have someone available to assist you with tasks such as cooking, cleaning, transportation, home maintenance, medication management, etc.?*

In a retirement community, staff is available to cook wonderful meals and clean your apartment for you. They're able to fix your broken refrigerator and repair the roof. By letting someone take over these tasks for you (if that's what you want), you now have more time to relax and do that socializing we were talking about in the previous section. However, if you enjoy doing those tasks (and many people do), then by all means continue to do them! For example, if you enjoy cooking, look for a community that provides kitchens in the apartments.

# The Path to Finding a Senior Living Community

Moving to a retirement community doesn't mean that you have to give up the activities that you enjoy. What it means is that you can choose what to do and what not to do – it's completely up to you and your preferences.

*The first time you visit a senior living community, I strongly suggest making an appointment with the marketer. That way, you'll be assured that someone has made the time in their schedule to spend with you. They'll be able to show you around, answer your questions, and even treat you to lunch!*

*With that being said, I do recommend visiting unannounced to see what the community is like when you're not expected. However, take that scheduled tour first.*

*Do you enjoy easy access to various forms of entertainment such as live music, outings, board and card games, special theme dinners, movies, educational speakers, etc.?*

A good retirement community will have many and varied activities of interest for you to participate in. Ask to see the monthly activity calendar and check it for activities that you enjoy. Also, look for activities that you've wanted to participate in or learn but haven't been able to for whatever reasons. Wii bowling seems to be popular, and some communities have teams that compete with other communities. They even have team shirts and trophies! There are fun trips available, outings to local casinos, opportunities to attend the theater, shopping, live music, happy hours, special dinners, arts & crafts, speakers and educational opportunities, choirs and thespian groups...the list goes on.

# The Path to Finding a Senior Living Community

*Do you want to consolidate your multiple bills every month, i.e. your utilities, food, home maintenance, transportation, entertainment, etc.?*

Quite often people are shocked when they hear the amount of monthly rent a person pays in a retirement community. It can be quite a high number. However, be aware that the cost is (almost) all-inclusive. For example, monthly rent usually includes meals, utilities, cable TV, housekeeping, some laundry services, transportation, outings, entertainment (happy hours, live bands, arts & crafts, games, etc.), apartment and grounds maintenance, 24-hour onsite/awake staff, utilization of all common areas (game room, pool, movie theater, bistro, etc.), and more. Ask the staff what the monthly rent includes.

*Feel free to attend some of the events that are offered at the community. Ask for an activity calendar and join in on an art class, an exercise class, free musical entertainment, and/or a meal in the dining room. This will give you the opportunity to experience community life first hand and to talk with some of the residents about their experiences at the community.*

*You don't need to be retired to move into a community, nor do you need to be independent (but you definitely can be). Do you need some assistance with Activities of Daily Living (ADLs)?*

Many communities have both independent residents (some still employed) and people needing some type of assistance living together. Some inter-mix everyone and others segregate the independent from the assisted in different areas of the community. A good question to ask when you visit communities is if they make someone change apartments when/if they change from being independent to assisted living.

# The Path to Finding a Senior Living Community

Also, some communities will allow you to spend a couple of nights with them to 'try out' the community and discover if you like the lifestyle. However, I want to caution you that a couple of days really doesn't give you the full taste of community living. You don't have the opportunity to make good friendships and explore all options available to you. For the majority of people that move into a retirement community, it takes three months or more before they really feel at home. However, once they do get their new routine and friendships established, they wonder why they didn't make the move sooner!

Be advised that a 55+ senior living apartment complex is not the same as a retirement community. A 55+ apartment complex, such as SHAG, doesn't provide extra amenities such as the ones that we've been talking about. Be sure to clarify when you're visiting different places.

# The Path to Finding a Senior Living Community

## Locate and Choose the Right Community

Now, more than ever before, there are many different retirement communities to choose from. How do you decide which one is the one for you? I want to make sure it's clear that we won't be discussing skilled nursing facilities (SNFs). SNFs are for people that need 24-hour skilled nursing care. A retirement community is for people who may need some assistance, but not round-the-clock nursing.

In the past, people would visit two or three retirement communities before choosing the one that they thought was right for them. These days, people are looking at five or more before making a decision. That's a lot of looking and touring! It can be very tiring and frustrating, especially for a senior. How can you make it simpler and easier?

One way is to research communities using the internet. You can get a basic idea of the community via the information that they share online but you should follow-up with a call to the community if it's one that you're interested in. Ask to speak with the Community Relations Director or the Sales & Marketing Manager. If the community looks and sounds good, make an appointment to visit! Retirement communities are more than just apartments; they're a lifestyle, and you really need to experience the lifestyle by viewing it firsthand.

Another option is to use a referral service. Be aware, however, that many referral services will only connect you with a community via a third person. In other words, they won't actually assist you as you work through the process of locating and choosing a community. One example of this is A Place for Mom (APFM). When you call A Place for Mom, they send your contact information to dozens of communities who will then start bombarding you with phone calls. The worst thing, in my opinion, is that APFM really doesn't know if the

# The Path to Finding a Senior Living Community

communities that they send your information to will be a good fit for you or not.

A third option is to use a placement company that will actually 'hold your hand' and be with you physically as you work through the process. They'll sit down with you, discover what you're looking for, narrow the field for you, and assist you as you visit the communities that you've chosen to look at. The placement company that you work with won't charge you a fee. Instead, the community you move into pays the placement company a fee. (Be sure to discuss fees and payment options at the first meeting, because things could have changed since the printing of this book).

The one downfall to using this service is that the placement company will only talk with, and show you, communities that they have contracts with. You could be missing out on a great community that they won't show you because there's no signed contract between the placement company and the retirement community.

What are some questions to ask and things to look for when you visit a community? The following are some questions that you may want to ask/consider:

Were you greeted promptly by the front desk staff and offered assistance?

As you tour the building, observe staff and resident interactions. Is the staff patient and kind? Were you greeted by residents and staff as you toured? Did you observe residents socializing with each other and/or attending activities? Ask a resident about their community experiences.

# The Path to Finding a Senior Living Community

Was there an activity calendar posted or is there one in the tour packet? If so, do any of the planned activities meet you or your family member's wants/needs?

Is the building clean and odor free?

Are the hallways, doorways, and common areas conducive for safe walking? Are the hallways wide enough and is there adequate lighting, are handrails and places to sit available, are common rooms free from area rugs and tripping hazards, etc.?

Take the time to have a meal. Is the service friendly and attentive? Are the dining hours and food choices flexible? Did the staff meet your food handling expectations?

Meet the General Manager and other key staff, if possible. (Due to meetings and responsibilities, this isn't always possible.)
How many staff members are scheduled throughout the day? Check on evening availability and a system for obtaining assistance 24-hours/day.

Ask about staff training and credentials. Is there a licensed nurse on staff? If so, how many hours per day or week is the nurse in the building?

Is the most recent state survey available for review?

What does your gut tell you?

You can also ask more specific questions such as the following:

How many staff are there for each shift?

# The Path to Finding a Senior Living Community

What are their responsibilities? For example, does the caregiving staff also perform housekeeping and dining room duties?

What is the training/certification of the caregivers?

What are the trainer's qualifications?

How many residents are assigned to each direct caregiver? Keep in mind that direct caregivers are needed for people who are on assisted living, not for independent residents. For people with dementia or Alzheimer's, are the caregivers trained to deal with behaviors? Check with your local HCS office to find out what your state considers the required training.

Are there direct care staff who speak English (or your native language) clearly? Is there special training for staff in regards to dementia and Alzheimer's disease? How long is the training?

Is staff trained to deal with aggressive individuals? Wanderers?

What if I don't like the staff person assigned to me/my loved one?

What is the staff turnover rate?

Emergencies:

Who decides to call 9-1-1?

Are there written policies about how that decision is made?

What kinds of emergencies are staff expected to handle and how are they trained for them?

# The Path to Finding a Senior Living Community

### How Do I Afford a Retirement Community?

Let's face it. It all comes down to cost in the end. You've found the community that you like and want to move into, but how are you going to pay for it? There are the obvious options such as savings, Social Security benefits, pensions (if you're lucky enough to have one), and money from the sale of a home. But will they be enough?

First, ask what the monthly rent at a retirement community includes. If you look at it item by item, it's usually more affordable than you think. In your home, you're most likely paying separately for utilities, garbage, cleaning supplies, food, entertainment, landscaping, home maintenance, property taxes, transportation, and more. In a retirement community, these items are typically included in your monthly rent.

If you or your spouse was in the military, you may qualify for VA benefits. Some communities also have their own in-house program for people with low incomes. If finances are extremely tight, there's your state Medicaid program. Many communities, however, don't accept Medicaid and you'll need assistance from your local home and community service office (HCS) to locate an appropriate community. There's also an Elderlife line of credit for senior living and, if you have it, long-term care insurance. Be sure to check with your long-term care insurance agency to find out what services it will pay for.

If you have a life insurance policy, look into the option of turning your policy into cash and using that cash to pay for your retirement community needs.

Don't forget to ask about entry fee costs, such as a buy-in fee or a community fee. Some communities will charge you hundreds of thousands of dollars to 'buy-in' to the community, while others charge a few thousand dollars. Then,

# The Path to Finding a Senior Living Community

check out the contract specifics, i.e. is it month-to-month rent or is there some other contractual obligation?

# The Path to Finding a Senior Living Community

## Comprehensive Assessment

Typically, before you move into a community, you'll complete some type of comprehensive assessment. Each state should have their own regulations. In Washington State, the Revised Codes of Washington (RCW) states in section 18.20.350:

Preadmission assessment—Initial resident service plan—Respite care.

(1) The assisted living facility licensee shall conduct a preadmission assessment for each resident applicant. The preadmission assessment shall include the following information, unless unavailable despite the best efforts of the licensee:

    (a) Medical history;

    (b) Necessary and contraindicated medications;

    (c) A licensed medical or health professional's diagnosis, unless the individual objects for religious reasons;

    (d) Significant known behaviors or symptoms that may cause concern or require special care;

    (e) Mental illness diagnosis, except where protected by confidentiality laws;

    (f) Level of personal care needs;

    (g) Activities and service preferences; and

    (h) Preferences regarding other issues important to the resident applicant, such as food and daily routine.

(2) The assisted living facility licensee shall complete the preadmission assessment before admission unless there is an emergency. If there is an emergency admission, the preadmission assessment shall be completed within five days of the date of admission. For purposes of this section, "emergency" includes, but is not limited to: Evening, weekend, or Friday afternoon

# The Path to Finding a Senior Living Community

admissions if the resident applicant would otherwise need to remain in an unsafe setting or be without adequate and safe housing.

(3) The assisted living facility licensee shall complete an initial resident service plan upon move-in to identify the resident's immediate needs and to provide direction to staff and caregivers relating to the resident's immediate needs. The initial resident service plan shall include as much information as can be obtained, under subsection (1) of this section.

(4) When a facility provides respite care, before or at the time of admission, the facility must obtain sufficient information to meet the individual's anticipated needs. At a minimum, such information must include:

(a) The name, address, and telephone number of the individual's attending physician, and alternate physician if any;

(b) Medical and social history, which may be obtained from a respite care assessment and service plan performed by a case manager designated by an area agency on aging under contract with the department, and mental and physical assessment data;

(c) Physician's orders for diet, medication, and routine care consistent with the individual's status on admission;

(d) Ensure the individuals have assessments performed, where needed, and where the assessment of the individual reveals symptoms of tuberculosis, follow required tuberculosis testing requirements; and

(e) With the participation of the individual and, where appropriate, their representative, develop a plan of care to maintain or improve their health and functional status during their stay in the facility.

If you don't have a primary care physician (PCP), or haven't been to see your PCP in a while, you'll need to schedule an appointment.

Once your care needs, if any, have been identified, take a look at the community's schedule of services and fees to determine if the community offers

# The Path to Finding a Senior Living Community

the specific services that you need. Talk with the nurse on staff to get your care need questions answered.

# The Path to Finding a Senior Living Community

### Selling a Home and/or Downsizing

You've located the community that you like and you've determined that you can afford to live there. Before (or during) your move into the community, you may need to do some downsizing.

Downsizing can be one of the most difficult, but also most liberating, aspects of your move. How do you decide what to keep, what to donate, what to give to family, and what to throw away? There are many downsizing professionals that can assist you with the process. They can also assist you with an estate sale and they know where to sell or donate your items so that you don't end up throwing something away that may be useful to someone else. Ask the Community Relations Director or Sales & Marketing Manager at the community for some referrals.

If you're selling a home, don't assume you must make costly repairs and improvements prior to listing your home. The right real estate agent will help you decide which repairs or improvements are necessary to increase your home value and reduce the time it takes to sell.

Also, never answer the question, "How much do you think your home is worth?" on your own. The first month your home is listed is the most important, and you don't want to be at the wrong price. A better method is to get a professional home inspection.

Finally, get a comprehensive competitive analysis from two or more real estate agents and compare them. Never rely only on one agent's opinion.

A website you can look at to locate assistance with planning a move is the National Association of Move Managers at https://www.nasmm.org/. All NASMM General Members have completed required courses in safety and

# The Path to Finding a Senior Living Community

ethics and are screened for insurance. However, as always, the marketing/salesperson at a senior living community will have referrals for you that are specific to your area. Usually, they've worked with these people in the past and know who can be trusted and who will do a good job meeting your needs.

*Know what furniture you'll be able to take with you when you move. I had one family pick out an apartment, pay their deposit, and start moving furniture into their new apartment. For some reason, the wife thought that she could move all the furniture from her 1400sf home into her 893sf apartment. When she found out that she couldn't, she and her husband decided to move back to their home. They were only in the community for six days! That was one expensive mistake.*

# The Path to Finding a Senior Living Community

### Integrate Yourself into the Community

Moving into a retirement community where others are already living can be scary! Some people have lived there for years and have established great friendships. Just remember that they were once new also.

One of the most important people to introduce yourself to is the Activity, or Life Engagement, Director. This is the person who is in charge of the majority of the activities and entertainment. Let this person know what you like to do for fun, and they should make sure that you're aware of the days and times that events you enjoy are happening. They can also introduce you to some other people that enjoy the same types of activities that you do.

The dining room can be a bit tricky. Even if there isn't assigned seating, people have their favorite tables where they enjoy eating. The Dietary Manager or Chef should be able to help you locate a table that works for you. If, for whatever reason, things don't work out at first, make sure that you bring it to the attention of the management. Their job is to assist you and make sure that you feel comfortable in your new home.

Also, don't be afraid to approach someone and introduce yourself. You never know, they might be new also.

*Recently, a new resident moved into the retirement community that I work for. After a few days, she came to my office crying. She was sad and anxious because she wasn't meeting anyone. I asked her what events and activities she'd been to. She told me, "none." She had been spending all her time alone*

# The Path to Finding a Senior Living Community

*in her apartment, waiting for people to come to her. In order to meet people, you need to make the effort to get out of your apartment and join in.*

# The Path to Finding a Senior Living Community

## The Emotional Aspects of Moving

Many seniors have lived in their homes for 40+ years. It can be extremely difficult to contemplate leaving behind the home where so many memories were made. Emotional stress can come into play and manifest itself with various symptoms such as:

- Fatigue
- Loss of Energy
- Decreased Socialization
- Loss of Interest
- Major Mood Changes

Some environmental clues that might be seen include:

- Unkempt Appearance
- Poor Hygiene
- Diminished Driving Skills
- Memory Loss
- Forgetfulness
- Confusion

These symptoms and environmental clues could also be signs that it definitely is time for a move to a senior living community. What can help an older person through this time in their life? A presentation by the American Society on Aging recommends the following:

Keep the brain active by reading, writing, doing crossword puzzles, Sudoku, and card games. If you're internet savvy, check out Posit and Lumosity online. To keep the body strong, get regular exercise (retirement communities provide exercise classes specifically for the older person), and strength training with light weights or Therabands. Spirituality can also be very important. Many

# The Path to Finding a Senior Living Community

retirement/assisted living communities provide opportunities for connecting with others spiritually.

Obtain an activity calendar from a retirement community that you're interested in and drop in on their programs so that you can give them a try. In this way, you'll experience for yourself how things really work in a community and you'll start to create the relationships that will make your move easier.

John Cacioppo, a psychologist at the University of Chicago, discovered in a study conducted by a group of researchers that loneliness increases a senior's risks of premature death and is, in fact, more deadly than obesity. While moving is difficult, it's better than living a lonely life.

An article titled 'Combating the Epidemic of Loneliness in Seniors' by AgingCare (https://www.agingcare.com/Articles/loneliness-in-the-elderly-151549.htm) states that "...despite advances in communications technology and the increasing connectedness it brings, research indicates that as a society, we are lonelier than we have ever been. Perhaps no other age group feels the keen sting of loneliness more than the elderly."

The article points out the fact that changes as we age contribute to a more solitary life. Changes such as social circles shrinking due to friends, family members, and significant others move away or pass away. Our mobility, cognition, and other physical factors may decline which leads to an inaccessibility of others (driving becomes unsafe, hearing loss leads to frustration and non-communication, low vision makes it unsafe to be out of the home at night, etc.). Embarrassment can also be a factor. Many older adults suffer from incontinence, use oxygen, or use a mobility device such as a wheelchair or walker.

A senior living community could be a great way to combat this loneliness.

# The Path to Finding a Senior Living Community

The Mather LifeWays Institute on Aging published The Age Well Study (https://www.matherlifewaysinstituteonaging.com/agewellstudy/). In this study, the authors state that, "...community residents tend to have greater life satisfaction than older adults from the community at large." They further state that, "...community residents have a positive outlook about the future," and, "...community participants have relatively low levels of loneliness, and residents are less lonely than older adults from the community at large."

# The Path to Finding a Senior Living Community

## Other Living Options

There are some other options that you may want to consider, especially if you've decided that a senior living community isn't for you.

Home health agencies can come into your home and provide services such as light housekeeping, cooking, transportation, companionship, medication assistance, basic wound care, etc. On a short-term basis (usually), you could qualify for an RN, physical and/or occupational therapy, speech therapy, etc. These services are usually prescribed by your MD and paid for with your Medicare B benefit. What the services can't provide is the social interaction and fun with others that you get in a senior living community. And, if you need a lot of care/assistance, this option can cost more than a senior living community.

Another option is an adult family home. This is when you or your loved one lives in a room in someone's private home. There are usually six people, at the most, living in the home. You may have to share a bedroom and a bathroom with others. Once again, these homes usually don't provide as much socialization or as many activities/events as one would get in a retirement community, nor do they provide the same amount of privacy. They can also be quite expensive.

You know what you're comfortable with, whether it's allowing someone into your private home, living in close quarters with others and sharing a bathroom with them, or living in an apartment-type dwelling. Look around, discover what's available, and decide what works best for you.

# The Path to Finding a Senior Living Community

### When Should you Start your Search?

I would suggest starting to check out your options *before* you need to make a move. Unfortunately, we don't know what life has in store for us, and it's best to have an idea of what's available before it becomes an emergency and a quickly needed move.

I've seen so many instances when someone has fallen or been in an accident, ends up in the hospital, is transferred to a rehabilitation facility, and then needs to find living options because it's not safe for them to return home. They're in pain, healing from an injury, worried about finances because insurance no longer pays for their hospital/rehabilitation stay, and have no idea where to go. Often, the children are required to make a quick decision about living arrangements when they themselves are working, raising kids, and dealing with their own life issues. It can be an extremely stressful situation, and often bad decisions are made because there's no time to make a good decision.

After someone is discharged from the hospital, the next move is often to a rehabilitation (rehab) facility. The hospital discharge planner usually sends your medical information to the local rehab facilities to find out who has a bed available and accepts your medical insurance. You are then transferred to that facility. But, what if that's not the facility where you want to be?

While you're well, before any accidents have occurred or a life changing health diagnosis has been received, go out and tour some of the local rehab facilities. Make a list of the facilities where you would feel comfortable and those that you don't want to be sent to. Make sure your family knows where you keep this list. If you end up in the hospital, share this information with your case manager/discharge planner.

# The Path to Finding a Senior Living Community

This works the same for senior living communities. If you can't return home after your stay at the hospital and/or rehab facility, you need to be able to let your family know which communities you would be comfortable with, and which to avoid. The only way to make this decision is to **visit the communities while you're well**.

# The Path to Finding a Senior Living Community

### Let the Fun Begin!

You've found the right senior living community and you've moved in. What now? Now, the fun begins...if you allow it to. What you shouldn't do is sit back and not participate in the life of the community. There are so many opportunities available to you at this point. Go back to the chapter titled 'Integrate Yourself into the Community.' Make an appointment to meet the Activity/Active Living Director and let them know what types of events you're interested in. Do you like to exercise, go to the movies, listen to live music, attend social hours, play board and card games? Make sure you know where and when the activities are taking place.

Also, introduce yourself to some of the people who already live in the community. Sit at different tables and with different people during meals. This is one of the ways that you'll get to meet others and find out who shares some of your interests and views about life.

It can take about three months or so to get acclimated to your new apartment and community. Give yourself time to settle in – don't expect it to happen overnight. This is an exciting new lifestyle that you're entering into, and it'll take some time to adjust. If you have any difficulties, speak with the staff.

Enjoy!

# The Path to Finding a Senior Living Community

## Additional Resources

https://www.caregiverstress.com/fitness-nutrition/get-mom-moving/

https://soundgenerations.org/

https://www.caregiverstress.com/senior-safety/health-information-management/

https://fivewishes.org/

https://www.homage.org/

https://snohomishcountywa.gov/1031/Senior-Information-Assistance

### Works Cited

"Age Boldly Consulting – Everett, Washington – Professional Services | Facebook." Facebook. N.p., n.d. Web. https://www.facebook.com/ageboldly/

"American Society on Aging | Developing Leadership, Knowledge, and Skills to Address the Challenges and Opportunities of a Diverse Aging Society." N.p., n.d. Web.

"The Department of Veteran Affairs Aid & Attendance Benefit." Aid and Attendance Benefit, Financial Aid. N.p., n.d. Web.

"Discover What Your Brain Can Do." Brain Games & Brain Training. N.p., n.d. Web.

# The Path to Finding a Senior Living Community

"Elderlife Financial Services : Line of Credit Loan for Senior Living & Care and Community Entrance Fees." Elderlife Financial Services: Line of Credit Loan for Senior Living & Care Community Entrance Fees. N.p., n.d. Web.

Hogan, Paul, and Lori Hogan. Stages of Senior Care: Your Step-by-step Guide to Making the Best Decisions. New York: McGraw-Hill, 2010. Print.

"Home | Life Care Funding." Life Care Funding. N.p., n.d. Web.

"Medicaid Home | Medicaid.gov." Medicaid Home | Medicaid gov. N.p., n.d. Web.

MetLife Mature Market Institute." MetLife Mature Market Institute. N.p., n.d. Web.

"Moving Forward, Inc. – Redmond, WA – Small Business | Facebook." Facebook. N.p., n.d. Web.

"Posit.com." Posit.com. N.p., n.d. Web.

"Welcome Visitors!" NAPGCM RSS. N.p., n.d. Web.

Cacioppo, John. "Psychologist John Cacioppo explains why loneliness is bad for your health." Accessed http://www.igsb.org/news/psychologist-john-cacioppo-explains-why-lonliness-is-bad-for-your-health/.